# Billy Graham

## *Reaching Out To The World*

### by Paul Westman

DILLON PRESS, INC.   MINNEAPOLIS, MINNESOTA

Library of Congress Cataloging in Publication Data

Westman, Paul
   Billy Graham: reaching out to the world.

   (Taking part)
   SUMMARY: A biography of Billy Graham, a North Carolinian evangelist whose message of hope and love has brought him world-wide following and fame.
   1. Graham, Billy, 1918-        —Juvenile literature. 2. Evangelists—United States—Biography—Juvenile literature. [1. Graham, Billy, 1918-
      . 2. Evangelists]I. Title.
   BV3785.G69W44            269'.2'0924  [B]  [92]                81-9912
   ISBN 0-87518-220-8                                             AACR2

Dillon Press, Inc., 242 Portland Avenue South
Minneapolis, Minnesota 55415

Printed in the United States of America

3   4   5   6   7   8   9   10   91   90   89   88   87   86   85

# BILLY GRAHAM

Billy Graham is the greatest evangelist of the twentieth century. He has brought the word of God to peoples and nations in all parts of the world. From London and Budapest to Bombay and Tokyo, more than 90 million people have come to hear his message. "My goal is to proclaim the gospel to as many people as possible and to build bridges of peace and friendship," says Graham.

Born on a farm near Charlotte, North Carolina, young Billy Graham heard evangelists such as Billy Sunday and Mordecai Ham. At sixteen his first spiritual rebirth changed him from a reckless youth to an earnest student of the Bible. He was ordained a Baptist minister and became a prominent leader of the Youth for Christ movement in the 1940s.

Beginning with his remarkably successful Los Angeles crusade in 1949, Billy Graham's fame as an evangelist spread worldwide. Reaching out to the world as a servant of God, he has made friends among people of widely different religious and political beliefs. Wherever he has gone, even in Communist nations, the people have responded to his message of hope and love in a spirit of peace and friendship.

When Billy Graham was four years old, his parents took him to see Billy Sunday. Sunday was an evangelist. That meant he was a minister without a church. Sunday traveled all over the country preaching the gospel at special services. Everywhere he went, he asked people to accept Christ as their savior. Many were moved by the power of Sunday's preaching. They came forward to declare their faith in Jesus.

Billy Graham heard Sunday speak in a big pine building in Charlotte, North Carolina. In the building there were thousands of wooden benches for people to sit on. There was no floor. Instead, the bare ground inside was covered with sawdust so thick that it got into Billy's

*Billy Sunday, whose fiery preaching impressed young Billy Graham.*

shoes. The smell of sawdust and new pine was everywhere.

Two men sat down next to Billy. They talked about Billy Sunday. "Mr. Sunday was once a big league baseball player," said one man.

"Yes," his friend replied. "He's a great athlete. Sometimes he runs across the platform and slides to the pulpit like a baseball player. That's how he starts his sermon. He doesn't do it all the time, though."

Soon Mr. Sunday appeared. Billy was disappointed when he only walked to the pulpit, instead of sliding.

Once Mr. Sunday began to speak, however, Billy changed his mind. Listening to him was ten times better than going to church. This preacher waved his arms and shouted. He climbed onto the pulpit and even onto the piano. Billy had never seen anything like it.

After Sunday left Billy had to listen to a preacher who wasn't nearly as exciting. The Grahams were a religious family. They went to church every Sunday. Mr. and Mrs. Graham believed that Sunday was the Lord's day. No work or play was allowed. For the Grahams, Sunday was a time for Bible reading and prayer.

Billy liked church well enough. But sometimes he could not understand the minister's words. Then he started to fidget. Once he fidgeted so much that Mr. Graham lost his temper. He did not even wait to get Billy home to give him a spanking. He just put him across his knee and spanked him in the church lobby.

Billy's father, Frank Graham, was strict. He believed in the saying, "Spare the rod and spoil the child." If Billy did something wrong, he got a licking. The same was true for Billy's little brother, Melvin, and his two sisters, Catherine and Jean.

William Franklin Graham, Jr., was born on November 7, 1918, on a farm near Charlotte, North Carolina. Because William Franklin was too long, his family called him Billy Frank.

*Six-month-old Billy Graham with his mother.*

In school most of his friends just called him
Billy.

Billy had trouble in school as well as in
church. He went to the Sharon School in
Charlotte. On his first day, Mrs. Graham fixed
a lunch. "Eat this at recess," she said.

The first recess was at ten o'clock that
morning. Billy quickly ate his lunch. He did not
know that the noon recess was two hours away.

When noontime came, he had nothing to eat. He went hungry the rest of the day.

By the end of the day, Billy was starving. Finally the bell rang, marking the end of school. Billy hurried out of the building. As he approached the door, the principal reached out and yanked his ear. Billy turned bright red. His ear smarted. He had no idea what he had done wrong. As far as Billy was concerned, school was going to be no fun at all.

From that day on, Billy was a poor pupil. He worked hard only at subjects he liked. "Why should I study?" Billy asked himself. "I'm going to be a farmer, and farmers don't need schooling."

Instead of studying, he was a prankster. One teacher had to chase him around the room and whack him with a ruler to settle him down. Another teacher kept Billy right next to his desk so that he could keep an eye on him. The only trouble he had was keeping Billy awake.

Billy was tired at school because work on the

Graham farm started very early each day. He and Melvin were up every morning at three o'clock. With their father, they milked the cows. Then Mr. Graham and the boys delivered the milk to homes in Charlotte. Three hundred customers bought their milk. That meant three hundred stops each morning. After school Billy had more chores. Sometimes he worked in the fields until sunset.

Billy found some time to play, too. Living on a farm helped. There were horses to ride, woods to play in, and streams to fish and swim in. There was also a big barn to climb around in.

For Billy reading was fun. Since he liked adventure stories, he read all the Tarzan books. Then he climbed the trees in the yard. Swinging from branch to branch, he yelled just like he thought Tarzan would.

History was Billy's favorite subject. As a boy, he read more than a hundred books about the great events of the past.

In a way, history was part of Billy's life. In

North Carolina the Civil War was still very real. People talked about it as if it had just happened. Actually, it had taken place more than sixty years before.

Billy's grandfathers had both fought for the South in the war. One of them, Grandfather Coffey, was tall, fair-haired, and blue-eyed— just like Billy. He had been wounded in Pickett's charge at the Battle of Gettysburg.

After the Civil War, blacks were freed from slavery. They could live and work where they wanted. One of the three farmhands who worked for Mr. Graham was a black man named Reese Brown. Reese was Billy's hero. He had been a sergeant in World War I. Reese was so big and strong that he could pin down a bull while other men removed its horns.

By the time Billy was ten, the farm was doing well. The Grahams had built a new red brick house near the old farmhouse. Mr. and Mrs. Graham had even saved a small sum of money. They kept it in a bank account.

Then, in 1929, the Depression swept the country. Many people lost their jobs and their homes. The Grahams' bank closed. Every penny of the Grahams' hard-earned money was lost.

*People waiting outside of a bank that failed during the Depression. Many lost all their savings.*

The Grahams were discouraged, but they did not believe in quitting. Soon, thanks to hard work and luck, they were able to make ends meet again. They kept their home and their farm.

Though Billy worked hard on the farm, he was still lazy in school. One day he did not show up for class. That made his teacher angry. "Billy Graham will never amount to anything," he said.

In high school Billy made trouble for just about everyone. He got into fights, and he drove Mr. Graham's car at high speeds down country roads. Once he became stuck in a mud hole. His father had to use a team of mules to haul the car out.

During his last year of school, one of Billy's teachers spoke to Mrs. Graham. "I am afraid Billy will not graduate," the teacher said. "This is a shame, because he is very bright. If he would only spend some more time at his schoolwork, he would have no problem at all."

In that same year a big change took place in Billy's life. It all started when an evangelist named Mordecai Ham came to town. Ham was a "fire and brimstone" preacher. His sermons were loud and lively. Thousands of people came from miles around to hear him.

Billy Graham was one of those who came to hear Mordecai Ham. Ham spoke to a packed crowd in a pine building. As he began to preach, Billy listened, spellbound. Mordecai Ham's preaching reminded him of Billy Sunday. Ham paced back and forth. He bent down on one knee. He yelled, shouted, and pointed at the Bible.

Suddenly Billy was seized with fright. Mordecai Ham pointed straight at him. "You're a sinner," Ham thundered. Shamed, Billy hid his head behind a woman's hat.

After the service, the crowd sang gospel tunes. One of the songs was "When the Roll Is Called Up Yonder." It went like this:

When the trumpet of the Lord shall sound
And time shall be no more
And the morning breaks eternal, bright,
and fair,
And the saved of the earth shall gather
Over on the other shore
And the roll is called up yonder,
I'll be there.

Billy was excited by the words of the gospel song. He was deeply moved by Mordecai Ham's preaching. Hundreds of others were moved, too. They stood up and walked to the altar.

"Come forward, accept your sins, and accept Christ," Ham urged. "God is calling you. He will never be so near again. Come forward, Brother. Come along, Sister. God bless you."

Billy stood up and joined the others. He knelt by the altar as the evangelist prayed.

That night Billy lay in bed, staring out the window of his room. A full Carolina moon shone through the window glass. He looked at it for a long time. Though he could not explain the strange feeling inside of him, he knew something wonderful had happened. Something had spoken to his heart.

Afterwards, Billy changed. He no longer acted wild, and his grades improved. In 1936 he finished high school with the rest of his class.

That fall Billy entered Bob Jones College in Tennessee. Bob Jones College was a strict religious school. Students were not allowed to dance, watch movies, or play cards. They could not even complain. A sign in the hall said "NO GRUMBLING ALLOWED."

Billy did not like Bob Jones College. He was not feeling well, either. To find out what was wrong, he went to a doctor. "What you need is sunshine," the doctor told him. Billy took the doctor's advice. He enrolled at the Florida Bible Institute in Tampa, Florida.

Students at the Bible institute all worked to help pay for their schooling. Billy washed dishes, cut grass, trimmed hedges, raked

*Billy Graham as a student at the Florida Bible Institute.*

leaves, and shined shoes. He earned twenty cents an hour for his work.

The founder of the Bible institute was Dr. W.T. Watson. Soon after Billy arrived, Dr. Watson called a meeting. All of the students and teachers were there.

"The institute is in deep trouble," Dr. Watson said. "If we do not get funds, the school will be forced to close. Let's pray to God for help."

Billy, Dr. Watson, and the others prayed. That night a note arrived along with a check for $10,000. The note said, "I felt strangely burdened to send this money to you." To Billy the gift was a miracle. It made him believe in the power of prayer.

At the institute Billy studied the Bible. One night a minister asked him to preach at his church. "But I don't know how to preach," Billy said.

"Give it a try," said the minister. "God will help you."

"I'll do my best," Billy replied.

Billy prepared four sermons. Each sermon was to last one hour. That way, if he finished too soon, he would still have plenty to talk about.

The night before he was to preach, Billy could not sleep. He paced the floor and prayed. The next day Billy faced forty people in a little clapboard church. His knees shook, and his hands dripped with sweat. In just eight minutes he went through all four sermons. Then he sat down, ashamed.

After that Billy was sure that God did not want him to preach. He took long walks, and he prayed for hours on end.

One night Billy was walking near the institute. Spanish moss hung from the trees. In the moonlight, the grounds were like a fairyland. All at once, Billy knew that God was calling him to preach. He dropped to his knees and prayed. "God, if you want me to preach, I'll do it," he said.

The trouble was, nobody else wanted him. No one asked to hear his sermons. Since Billy had nowhere else to go, he went to Franklin Street.

Franklin Street was the most sinful street in the city of Tampa. It was filled with drunks, gamblers, and thieves. There Billy preached at street corners and in front of saloons. He preached at the Tampa City Mission. Often he was booed and laughed at. Once a gang of toughs threw him into a gutter.

*Children's Bible Mission students with their young teacher, 19-year-old Billy Graham (far right, back row).*

Billy had trouble with words. Sometimes people laughed out loud when he didn't say them right. Their laughter embarrassed him.

He had other problems, too. His Carolina accent was too thick. He talked too loud and too fast, and he waved his arms. "Billy looks like a preaching windmill," people joked.

Every mistake Billy made caused him to try harder. To learn more about words, he bought an old set of encyclopedias and read straight through them. He practiced and prayed so hard by day that often he could not sleep at night.

To improve his speaking, Billy went to a cypress swamp by the river. Using a stump for a pulpit, he preached to the birds and the alligators. That way he could practice without being laughed at.

Soon Billy's sermons began to be taken seriously. Churches in many Florida towns were asking to hear the "boy preacher," as he was known. After each sermon Billy invited people to come forward and accept Christ. At one small church 32 men and women came forward. The Sunday school director had a high opinion of young Billy Graham. "There's a young man who will be known around the world!" he exclaimed.

As Billy continued preaching, he thought about becoming a minister. He had been raised as a Presbyterian church member. In 1939, however, he decided to become a Baptist. Members of the local Baptist church led Billy to a beach at Silver Lake where he was baptized. In that same year Billy became a Baptist minister. He was only twenty years old. From that moment on, he was the Reverend Billy Graham.

In 1940 Billy Graham graduated from the Florida Bible Institute and entered Wheaton College in Illinois for more schooling. Illinois and the north were foreign to the young minister. His clothes were out of style, and he could not afford new ones. He had a hard time making friends.

All that changed when Billy met a young woman named Ruth Bell. Ruth, too, was a student at Wheaton. She had been born in China, where her parents worked as missionaries. Before long Billy and Ruth became close friends. Two years later, in 1943, they were married.

After college Billy became the pastor of the First Baptist Church in Western Springs, Illinois. Western Springs is a suburb of Chicago.

Graham changed the name of the church to The Village Church. Changing the name, he hoped, would open up the church to other people besides Baptists. Graham believed that hearing God's word was more important than belonging to a certain kind of church.

A Baptist pastor named Torrey Johnson heard Billy Graham speak. Reverend Johnson had a radio program of preaching and gospel singing called "Songs in the Night." The program was broadcast each Sunday evening from Chicago.

Johnson asked Billy Graham to take over the program. Graham was surprised and pleased by the offer, and he asked his church members to help raise funds to support the broadcasts. Soon "Songs in the Night" was being broadcast from The Village Church. It was a big hit with Chicago radio listeners. Many sent letters to Graham saying how much they liked his program.

"Songs in the Night" was so successful that

Johnson asked Billy Graham to try something new. As a result of World War II, thousands of servicemen were coming into Chicago each weekend. Many of them spent their time drinking, gambling, and getting into trouble. Johnson wanted to bring religion to these young people.

To get their attention, Johnson organized a big event. He rented a large meeting hall which held three thousand people. Then he asked all the servicemen to come to a "Youth for Christ" rally.

Johnson asked Graham to preach at the rally. At first Graham was not sure. Finally he agreed to speak. When he saw the packed hall, however, he was seized with stage fright. He had never spoken to such a large crowd in his life. As soon as he started talking, his fear left him. Billy Graham believed that God gave him the strength to preach about Jesus. He wanted everyone to know and share his belief that Christ is the light of the world.

The Youth for Christ movement spread from Chicago to other cities. Graham spoke at rallies all over the United States and in Europe. Before long a thousand Youth for Christ groups had sprung up around the world.

In 1949 Graham held a crusade in Los Angeles. For the young minister, a crusade was a campaign to bring God's message to many people in one city or country. In Los Angeles Graham spoke in a huge tent where evangelists came to hold religious meetings. In fact, the tent could hold more people than the big pine building in Charlotte where Graham had gone to hear Billy Sunday.

At first the people of Los Angeles did not know who the tent preacher was. But as the days went by, the crowds grew larger and larger. Even though the tent held thousands of people, many had to be turned away.

Graham spoke as loud as he could so that even the people outside the tent could hear him. He paced back and forth on the platform. He

*A crowd gathers outside the huge tent where Billy Graham held the Los Angeles crusade in 1949.*

rose up onto his toes. He jabbed his finger in the air and clenched his fists. And he held the Bible in his hands.

Many people were moved by Billy Graham's fiery preaching. Once, when he was only halfway through his sermon, a man ran down the aisle. Tears streamed down his cheeks. "Please allow me to accept Christ right now!" he cried. "I can't stand it any longer!" Graham stopped his sermon. One of his church counselors prayed with the man and read to him from the Bible. On each day of the crusade, hundreds of people came forward to accept Christ as their savior.

The Los Angeles crusade was supposed to last three weeks. But so many people wanted to hear Billy Graham that he kept preaching for eight weeks. On the last night, seats for nine thousand people were set up inside and outside of the tent. The crowds were so large that they blocked traffic on nearby streets.

After the Los Angeles crusade, Billy Graham's

fame grew. Newspapers and magazines ran stories about him and the people who had changed their lives because of his preaching. Graham spoke to large crowds in Boston and many other cities. Soon he had requests to preach all over the world. There were so many requests that it was hard for Graham to keep up with them all. He didn't want to make promises that he could not keep.

One of the requests came from two Chicago businessmen. They asked Graham to go on the air with a nationwide Sunday afternoon radio program. All he needed, said the men, was $25,000 to pay for the first few weeks of the broadcasts. Graham said he was too busy to take on a weekly radio program. Besides, where would he get all the money to pay for it? The businessmen refused to give up. Again and again, they came back and asked him to go on the radio.

Finally Graham asked the men to join him in prayer. "If I get $25,000 by midnight, I'll go on

*Billy Graham in prayer.*

the air," he said. Graham did not believe that he would receive such a large sum of money. If he did, he believed it would be a sign from God to go on the air.

That night Billy Graham spoke before a large crowd at a crusade in Portland, Oregon. At the end of the meeting, he told the crowd about the radio offer. If the money was pledged that night, he said, he would start the weekly program. A few hours later, Graham found out that $23,500 had been given to the radio fund. He could hardly believe his ears. They were only $1,500 short.

When Graham returned to his hotel, the desk clerk handed him three letters. He opened them, and inside were three checks adding up to $1,500. That made a total of exactly $25,000.

Soon the new weekly radio program was on the air. Ruth Graham gave it its name—"The Hour of Decision." Within five years more than eight hundred stations around the world carried "The Hour of Decision." Millions of people listened to it, and it is still going strong today.

Billy Graham's fame as an evangelist spread to every corner of the earth. He spoke in Italy, Germany, France, Japan, Korea, and Argentina. In 1954 he traveled to England for the Greater London crusade.

At first newspapers and magazines in London made fun of him. They called him a "Hollywood preacher" and talked about "Billy Graham's American hot gospel circus." Graham knew that many people read the newspapers and magazines. He feared that after reading these stories, they would not come to hear him preach.

On the night of his first sermon, though, the arena was packed. Over the three months of the crusade, he spoke to standing room only crowds. In homes, factories, and clubs, Londoners talked about Billy Graham. Every night singing could be heard in the subway stations. "What a friend we have in Jesus," sang the

*At a crusade in Seoul, Korea, Billy Graham spoke to a crowd of more than one million people.*

riders as they waited in line for their tickets.

Graham spoke to more than 2 million people in London. So many English men and women wanted to hear him that the British Broadcasting service relayed his sermons to other cities. Even the press praised Graham for giving new life to religion in England. And at the end of the crusade, he met with Prime Minister Winston Churchill.

Two years after his visit to London, Billy Graham went to India. The crusade began in Bombay, India's largest city. From there it moved to Madras in the south where most of the country's Christians lived.

Most Indians believe in the Hindu religion. In Madras, however, many Hindus wanted to see Graham just as much as the Christians did. One of the Hindus who saw Graham told how he felt about his visit. "We watched Billy Graham when he was preaching and when he was just talking to people. He was always smiling. He was so happy. The thing he has fills him

*Billy Graham prays with children in southern India.*

with such joy that we want whatever it is he has, and he says Christ can give it to us."

Graham loved the colorful sights, striking sounds, and graceful people of India. Most of all, he liked to spend time with the children. He was saddened, though, by the many poor people who had little to eat. Everywhere he went, he tried to leave them with a message of hope and love. Often he ended his sermons with these words from the Bible, John 3:16. "God so loved the world, that he gave his only begotten son, that whosoever believeth in him should not perish, but have everlasting life."

Despite his worldwide travels, Billy Graham continued to preach in America, too. Each year he held four crusades in large sports stadiums or arenas.

By this time Graham had gathered a hard-working team to help at each crusade. Team members worked with local church groups to organize the events. Many people offered to counsel those who came forward at the end of

*A packed crowd gathered in a stadium to hear Billy Graham at his 1963 Los Angeles crusade.*

Graham's sermons. Others helped to find churches for those who accepted Christ.

Graham knew that his work was just the beginning of a change in people's lives. Local churches of all kinds were needed to follow up on what he had started. It wasn't easy for a person to make a big change in the way he or she lived. Worshipping together and sharing problems with other church members helped to make it less painful.

In 1958 Graham returned to Charlotte for a crusade in his hometown. Before the crusade Graham stayed at his parents' farm home. By now the city of Charlotte was growing up around it. The fields Billy used to plow were gone, and a shopping center had taken their place. There was an office building in the cow pasture. The Grahams even had a city address—4501 Park Road.

The Charlotte crusade worried Graham. Would people in his hometown listen to what he had to say? Would anyone come forward when he gave the call at the end of his sermon? And would whites and blacks be able to worship together in peace?

For five years Graham had refused to hold a crusade in which blacks and whites could not join in worship. In the 1950s many whites treated blacks as second-class citizens. In the South blacks sat in the back of the bus and on the far side of the stadium. Billy Graham believed human beings should not be treated that way. According to Graham, the Bible does not say that whites are any better than blacks or any other race. "Jesus Christ belongs to all races," he said. "There are no color lines with Christ. God looks upon the heart."

On opening night more than fourteen thousand people filled the arena. Blacks and whites sang gospel songs and prayed together. Then Billy Graham began to preach. At the end of his sermon, he bowed his head and asked people to come forward.

*At the end of his sermons, Graham asks people to come forward and accept Christ.*

No one moved. The only sound was the low humming of the choir. The silence went on and on. It was one of the longest waits Graham had ever gone through.

At last a frail old woman stood up. Holding a handkerchief to her eyes, she walked down the aisle. Others stood up and came forward, too. Four hundred people accepted Christ under Graham's ministry that day. He said later, "Charlotte was one of my best crusades."

Before each crusade, Billy Graham spent time at his home in Montreat, North Carolina. Billy and Ruth lived in a small log house high in the Blue Ridge Mountains. They had five children now: Virginia, Anne, Ruth, Franklin, and Nelson. At Montreat Graham read the Bible and prayed. To train his body, he walked or jogged along the winding mountain trails.

Billy Graham was still as eager to learn as he had been in the cypress swamps of Florida. Wherever he went, he carried a suitcase full of books. When others took their lunch break,

*Billy and Ruth Graham (center, sitting) with their five children, sons-in-law, and grandchildren.*

*Billy Graham preaching at a presidential prayer breakfast in 1963. Former presidents John F. Kennedy (left) and Lyndon B. Johnson (right) are listening.*

Graham studied. He even read on planes and trains. Often he studied six to eight hours a day between sermons and meetings with church leaders.

Because Graham was so well known, presidents asked for his advice on religious matters. He has won the respect of Harry Truman, Dwight Eisenhower, John Kennedy, Lyndon Johnson, Richard Nixon, Gerald Ford, Jimmy Carter, and Ronald Reagan. Members of Congress have invited him to hold crusades in

Washington, D.C. At the first crusade Graham held a special service on the steps of the nation's Capitol. It was broadcast live on radio and TV across the country.

Billy Graham has been invited to hold crusades in many countries. In 1967 he held one that had a special meaning for him. That year he was asked to preach in Yugoslavia, a Communist country in Eastern Europe.

Communist leaders do not approve of religion. Many try to keep their people from going to church and hearing the word of God. Christians and people of other religious faiths are treated as second-class citizens.

In Yugoslavia Graham spoke to an eager crowd of Christians and non-Christians in the city of Zagreb. The people stood in an open field in a pouring rain to hear him. Roman Catholic and Orthodox church leaders took part in the worship service. During the service everyone joined hands in an unbroken circle to sing and worship together.

*Billy Graham speaking to a large crowd near Budapest, Hungary.*

Ten years later, Billy Graham went to Hungary, another Communist country. He preached at a campsite on a hillside above the Danube River. Thirty thousand people—old peasants in homespun clothing and city youths in jeans— were there to hear him. They came from all over

*After a church service in Budapest, Graham signs an autograph for a young boy.*

Eastern Europe and even from the Soviet Union. At the close of the service, Graham asked all those who accepted Christ to raise their hands. Thousands in the packed crowd showed their hands.

Over the years, Billy Graham has brought the word of God to peoples and nations in all parts of the world. In 1980 he traveled to Japan for a nationwide crusade, and in 1981 he went to Mexico. More than 90 million people have come to hear his message. "My goal is to proclaim the gospel to as many people as possible and to build bridges of friendship and peace," says Graham.

That is exactly what he has done. Everywhere he has gone, people have come forward to accept Christ. Even in Communist nations, they have come in peace and friendship. Billy Graham remembers a worker in a national park in Hungary. With tears of joy in his eyes, he grabbed Graham's arm and said, "I am a believer!"

Billy Graham has been praised by presidents and prime ministers, bishops and popes. He has made many friends among people of different religious and political beliefs. And yet, through all his travels he has remained a servant of a power far greater than his own. "The work has been God's and not man's," says Graham. "I want no credit or glory. I want the Lord Jesus to have it all."

## The Author

Paul Westman is a regular contributor to *Current Biography* and has written many books for young people, including several for the Taking Part series. Of the series, Westman says, "Young readers will learn something about well-known contemporary men and women in many challenging fields and at the same time begin to discover some of the joys of reading."

A recent graduate of the University of Minnesota, Westman lives in Minneapolis.

*The photographs are reproduced through the courtesy of the Billy Graham Evangelistic Association, the Archives of Labor and Urban Affairs, Wayne State University, and the Religious News Service.*